D1500139

Birdsong

BROOKE ADKINS

Illustrations by Jenn Evans

Published by:
On The Go Talent LLC
onthegotalent.com

ISBN-13: 978-1-7376891-1-9

Production by Gary A. Rosenberg
www.thebookcouple.com

Illustrations by Jenn Evans

Printed in the United States of America.

To my RF Sistahs, Lisa and Sandy,
who encouraged me every Friday night
to share my poems.

Contents

"Once upon a time, when women were birds,
there was the simple understanding that
to sing at dawn and to sing at dusk
was to heal the world through joy.
The birds still remember
what we have forgotten,
that the world is meant to be
celebrated."

—Terry Tempest Williams

Author's Note

"Our fingerprints don't fade
from the lives we touch."

—JUDY BLUME

When I wrote "Robins' Return" and read it to my dear friend Sandy in November 2020, I had no idea how significant it would be to her. My illustrator had already suggested incorporating my fingerprints into the drawings of the birds, which I thought was a lovely idea.

After reading the poem to Sandy, she told me that after her son, Keegan, was laid to rest on a cold November in Saskatchewan, a Robin lighted nearby. She knew it was him. Hearing that, I decided to dedicate "Robins' Return" in memory of Keegan. Look closely at the Robin's red breast; you will see Keegan's thumbprint.

Robins' Return

As the rain drizzles down and the morning slowly begins,
Dozens of birds seek shelter in the tree,
Shaking off the droplets with spasms of joy,
In the dimness of the day, the shadows of the tree,
I can't tell who they are until . . .
Dozens of Robins gather in the yard,
Ah, you have returned, you have found me.

Blue Jay

You are beautiful, strong and powerful,
As you glide your way to the highest branches,
Sleek feathers of brilliant blue adorn your wings of
    free flight;
A setting of sapphire among the dull shade of the tree,
And then, instead of a melody that matches your
    outward beauty
Comes a squawking, cackling cry;
Belligerent, fighting ugliness that reveals your true
    inward;
Dominating, intimidating Blue Jay.

Hawk

The world that surrounds me is waking
From a humid stillness that foretells
A hot, violent, stormy day.
Not a breath of wind or a birdsong in the air,
Lazy lizards, daring dragonflies and
The incessant maddening sound of cicadas
Fill the space.
I hear her before I see her;
That familiar, woeful cry that identifies
Her presence for me to look upward.
Then I see her soaring majestically,
Circling, circling the tallest pine
Whose stature suits her.
She is crying out again, beating her wings
Furiously, circling, circling,
Issuing a warning, "Don't come near!"
Crying to her babies, "I will protect you!"
Later, she comes to me, silently
Perched on the fence post; mottled and
speckled plumage, strong bright-yellow
Talons; Hawk-eyed stare,
She brings a message to me.

Ibis

Ibis, ancient bird; I wonder how you got from Egypt
    onto my lawn!
Early morning riser; flocking with your fellow birds,
Your curved, orange saber stabbing the ground for
    some grub.
You were a god; revered, worshipped
As a sacred symbol.
Tropical, hot-white commoner now,
Belying your past,
Spearing the grass.

Little Wren

Good morning, little Wren, little Wren
Perched on the wire,
A cloudless sky, a gentle breeze,
Sweet song, you never tire
From singing sweetly, calling, chirping:
"I'm the morning crier!"
An audience has gathered, gathered now
To share the song.
Cacophony of pure delight,
No thought of right or wrong.
A twittering, cheeping, trilling Anthem
"Here's where we belong."
Now the choir assembly flits away
To other spots,
Soaring, darting, scanning, flying
Free from any thoughts
Of being only being little Wrens
That G-D has wrought.

Mockingbird

I hear a song in the morning,
As the pressure of humid heat bears down on the day,
The song is clear and seems familiar, calling out to me,
Then, it changes; a different refrain I try to recall,
Again and again, song after song,
Yet, from the same voice, the same location,
Why are you mocking me?
Mocking and confusing me into
 Thinking you are something you are not?
What is your true voice? Your true song?
Maybe you don't know yourself,
Mockingbird.

Parula

Chip, chip, chippy birds
Chip away at the morning silence.
I hear them before I see them
Flitting through the branches
Of the old water oak
Whose necks are draped carelessly
With scarves of Spanish moss.
Tiny Parulas; perfectly proportioned
To hide their presence through
The branches and the leaves.
Feather coat of blue-black, gray-green
Gives them shelter from a searching eye
Amid the lichen and shadows of the tree.
Hop, hop, hoppy birds,
Happy to glean whatever the oak has
To give,
Pretty little Parulas singing
Good morning to me.

Treasure Trove

It's a cloudy, balmy morning with a hint
Of summer breeze.
A congregation of cackling Blackbirds
Gather for their morning meal
In the yard; scavenging, probing for a tidbit,
Finding little to satisfy their hunger.
A lonely bird makes a discovery!
There is an aroma, a hint of hidden treasure
Buried inside a small, black hill in the yard.
Peck, peck, pecking away like a miner digging
For coal.
Success! A morsel, a
Meal and now, a melee of squawking,
All atwitter to get the chance for a peck and
A bite.
A lonely bird takes flight to the roof,
To enjoy a feast of fetid food,
Strutting and staying away from the
Raucous crowd.
Just as quickly as the morning parishioners
Gathered for their Eucharist,
They flew away in a murmuration of
Satisfaction.

Hummingbird

The rain has come; steady shower through the sunshine,
Leaves on the bushes flutter like hummingbirds hovering
    the branches.
Iridescent green, shiny bright.
Siphoning the sweet nectar that sustains their frantic
    flight.
I watch the rare sighting with a calm delight,
Unlike their nervous energy.
The rain subsides and the hummingbirds have gone.

Cardinal Angel

Consuming silent sounds of isolation
Noisy thoughts of past regrets
And lost moments fill the spaces
Between a crowded expanse of loneliness.
Think, don't think; do, don't do; Be.
Then, there's a Cardinal in the tree
A soft crimson bullet,
Darting, resting, peering down,
Twittering a familiar song that says,
"I'm here watching over you
So you'll know everything will be OK."
Just then another, less brilliant bullet of feathers lights
    nearby.
She sings, "I'm here for you, too; you're not alone."

With Gratitude

I am ever grateful to my "coach," Caryn Lutz, who had a vision for me: Brooke Writes Books! She held my hand and took me through the process step-by-step. Caryn also brought those in my life to make this journey a reality . . . My illustrator, Jenn Evans, who saw the uniqueness in my birds and brilliantly brought them to life.

My publishing team, Carol and Gary Rosenberg, who patiently waited for me and took me into their fold.

Influencers and resources known and unknown who inspired me: Mark Nepo, whose Book of Awakening brought me from the depths to a place of clarity; Todd Palmer, poet and colleague; and Kate Cuminsky, author and poet. I am grateful for your encouragement. The National Audubon Society Field Guide to North American Birds: Eastern Region was my "go-to" resource for identifying my backyard birds. Many friends encouraged me, love me, and suffered through my process: Lisa and Sandy; Heather Alexander, who is my bird guide; Jonathan Adkins, my spiritual Cuz; and my "work wife," Heather Gleason, who never wavers in her belief in me.

Last but not least, I am grateful for my family: my son, Thad Chapman; his wife, Nicole; and my grandchildren, Maria, Dominic, and Eva. My mother, Lynne Tracy; "Bonus Mom" Wanda Self; son and "Bonus Son" Andy Chapman and Aaron Robin (how befitting his name)!

About the Author

Brooke Adkins, most notably known as "Miss Brooke," lived in Port Orange, FL, with her backyard birds, until a recent move to Daytona Beach, FL. Born and raised in Huntington, WV, she can't remember not dancing. Her passion and talent for Ballet continued at The Academy of the Washington Ballet in Washington, D.C. where she graduated from high school. Under the direction of Mary Day, Brooke performed in the Washington Ballet's production of The Nutcracker, as a student performer. She also performed at Wolf Trap Farm Park in Vienna, VA, in the musical *Kismet*.

Brooke returned to Huntington and attended Marshall University, where she was cast as Maria in the dream ballet of the musical *West Side Story*, and taught ballet at local dance studios. Life and circumstances led to many career paths: medical assistant in WV, Human Services Technician and Crisis counselor in GA, preacher's wife, and mother.

Following God's "calling" for her ex-husband, Brooke became a Certified Ophthalmic Technician in IN and KY and continued that career in Florida. Again, circumstances afforded Brooke the opportunity to complete her post-secondary education and she earned her Regents' B.A. degree from Marshall University in 2002. She was hired by Volusia County Schools in 2003 as a permanent substitute teacher and then became the Dance Educator at Spruce Creek High School in Port Orange, FL, in 2004, where she has been teaching dance ever since.

All along this path, Brooke taught ballet in the private studio environment and has become a well-known ballet instructor. She is a member of the National Dance Educators' Organization and the Florida Dance Educators' Organization, and she sponsors a chapter of the National Honor Society of Dance Arts at Spruce Creek High School. Brooke is the director of the dance team at school (The Papillon Dance Ensemble), and teaches International Baccalaureate Dance.

Brooke is also an entrepreneur as an independent skin-care consultant. She has two grown children, Thad and Andrew Chapman, and three grandchildren, Maria Nichols, Dominic, and Eva Grace Chapman, who live nearby.